My Healing Journey

JoLynn Backes

Presentation by *BookLeaf Publishing*

Web: www.bookleafpub.com

E-mail: info@bookleafpub.com

ISBN: 978-93-95969-31-4

First edition 2022

DEDICATION

To all those who are on their own healing journey and all those who have assisted me in mine!

The Journey

Healing is not a destination, but a journey
It is this journey I propose
I am not the guide or the technical assistant
I will be your fellow passenger
Let's work together
To paint gold into our wounds
Share the highs
And lift each other up from the lows
Each step forward will bring new tools and new
wonders
Let's gather flowers when we're detoured
And pave new paths for fellow travelers
We'll move with grace and love
Creating a new, magnificent world as we go
It will not be easy,
But nothing worthwhile ever is
There will be times when we take a step forward
And are pushed back two
We will not relent
We will remain steadfast in our journey
We will remember that to keep on our healing path
We simply need to take
That next step

Journey Part II

May you be able to journey to
That place in your soul
Where there is great love, warmth,
Hope, and forgiveness
Take away the shame and self blame
The would've, could've, should'ves
Give yourself grace
Let the fiery anger dim
To the warmth of acceptance
Forgive yourself for doing
What you needed to do to survive
Forgive those who couldn't be there for you
And those who can't seem to understand
Feel the joy and freedom
That comes from knowing
You are special and deserving
Feel the strength of knowing
You are a survivor

Who Am I?

Who am I?
I can give the usual list:
Daughter, wife, mother, niece, aunt,
Cousin, granddaughter, friend
I can tell you what I do:
I am an advocate, supporting others
Through the darkness
I can list my hobbies:
Reader, writer, dancer
But will these titles and terms
Truly describe who I am
Will it let you know
That my trauma made me softer, not harder
Will it show you all the love I have inside
The compassion and empathy
That leave me weeping at times
I yearn to leave my mark on the world
I want to leave a legacy behind
One where when I am thought of
People will say I made the world
A better place
I am someone who embraces life
And embraces others
I am someone who strives
To do the right thing
And is terrified of doing the wrong thing
I am like the duck
Seemingly calm above water

All the while paddling like hell underneath
I am someone who worries she is
Not good enough
And never will be
I am the strong one
The one keeping everyone else afloat
Never wondering if I'm getting pulled under
I am the rock, the burden holder,
The confidant
I am the one everyone turns to
But who won't reach out to others
For fear of being a burden
I am the smile to brighten your day
The positive words to ease your pain
The encouraging hand to hold
Who am I?
Are you willing to peel back the layers and see?

Colors of My Pain

The colors of my pain have
Evolved over time
A kaleidoscope of shades and emotions
At the beginning there was gray
A swirl of confusion
Too young to know what was going on
And what to do
As the confusion turned to clarity
Gray turned to red and orange
A fire of rage burned within me
An all encompassing anger
At those who failed me
At myself for whatever I had done
To deserve this
At a system who protects those who harm
In order to not let the flames consume me
I let in blue
Water to douse the flames
And ice to numb the pain
The intense heat turned to unbearable cold
I was too numb to even feel joy
Chilled and shivering,
I reached out to purple
My favorite color of all
I let it wrap me in its
Calm and soothing presence
Cracks in the ice allowed more colors
To flood in

Yellow for the sun and green for the earth
I became grounded and
Experienced a rebirth
I allowed all the colors
To bathe me in their rays
Careful not to let in
Too much of any one color
Now I use these colors
To form a rainbow
Showing others it's ok
To sit with whatever color
They are in right now
To keep going
And collect a rainbow of their own

Someone Hear My Call

Why Won't Anyone Come?
I call --
But there is no answer
Why doesn't anyone hear me?
Where are they?
I don't know what to do and I'm all alone
I call out --
No one
I search --
No one
I sit in the darkness
Searching and calling
But there is no one

Rain

Rain go away
And with you drive away
The darkness that grips my heart
Let me breathe free for awhile
Rain please go away
And free me of the hurt and pain
And let the sun in me shine through

Rain II

Rain pours down my window endlessly
The drops fall in sync with my tears
The hot rain clouds my window
And I can only see darkness
Someone please help me see again
Someone please stop the rain
Someone please stop my tears

Grieving

I have and continue to grieve
I grieve my lost innocence
The space hurt and betrayal
Take up in my psyche
I grieve for lost time
Time spent crying instead of laughing
Shrinking into myself instead of growing
Being afraid and angry instead of free
I grieve the detour
My life was sent in by force
Were any of the choices I made my own
What path would I have gone down
If the earth hadn't opened up
And devoured it
What would that little girl have become
What would her life be like
If her heart wasn't torn apart
Relationships severed, new ones formed
Weaknesses exploited, strength found
Would that little girl recognize
The woman I've become

Mask

I hide behind my mask
Too afraid to take the chance
To let people see the real me
Too afraid of the rejection
Too afraid of the pain
So I sit here
Lonely as ever
Behind my mask
Losing my identity
Losing my being

Too Much

Too much pain
For such a little heart
A painful secret too terrible to tell
Too much hurt
For one person to take
Pain strong enough to kill
But never again will it get me
This time I will overpower it
With the support of a thousand others
In the same fight
For freedom and justice

Starting Anew

You're gone
And the pain is healing
Now I can finally start anew
I can put the pieces of my life
Back together
New friends help me
Start out in a new direction
To close a door on the past
A door that shall never again be opened

The Door

There's a door
That will lead you past the hurt and pain
All the scars, all the guilt
There's a door
That will lead you to comfort and healing
Bathe you in new light
New self and new purpose
There's a door
That will lead to beauty and wonder
Joy and peace
There's a door
That will lead you down a new path
There's a door
You just have to steady yourself
Take a deep breath
And walk through

Breaking Free

I will break the shell
Struggle free from the cocoon
I wove around myself
Take the pain and the fear
The doubt and the shame
Turn it into a sharp blade
I will move away from the darkness
Into the light
I have nothing to hide
I will not be contained anymore
I will show the world my strength
Inspiring others along the way
I will break the shell
And learn to fly

Butterfly

Little caterpillar consumed by the dark
Fearing your life is over
Not knowing where to go
You buried yourself and hid
Not wanting them to see your pain
Comforted by the dark
And the stillness within
You form your protective cocoon
Never letting anyone in
Tired of the dark
Ready to break free
Come into the light
Show your resilience
Let everyone see your transformation
Now a beautiful butterfly

Every Step I Take

Every step I take
The vise around my heart loosens
I am learning to breathe again
Every step I take
I become more confident in who I am
I am no longer afraid
The shame and anger are gone
Replaced by grace, love, and understanding
I am reaching out
Turning towards the sun
Every step I take
I am moving from
Surviving to thriving

I Am

I am love and forgiveness
I hear the cries of others and work to calm their
fears
I see the world as it could and should be
I taste the salty tears as they flow down
I touch hearts and minds
Struggling to change the culture
I smell the fire of phoenixes rising

I am love and forgiveness
I see peace and justice
I experience fulfillment in reaching out to others
I believe in a better world
Dream of one without violence
I am love and forgiveness

Journey Part III

It's taken many twists and turns
Detours and road blocks
There was no map
No paved path
I might have gotten lost in a dark forest
But I found a light
And blazed a new trail
I found my way
And am here where I am supposed to be
A survivor renewed

One Voice

Alone -
One voice in the night
One voice that is making a difference
It cries out to others in distress
To let them know there's hope
It pleads with them
To continue its search for a better world
A world thousands of others are striving for
It cries out one last time
I listen - And realize the voice is my own

Let Your Voice Ring Out

Someone, somewhere will hear your story
And decide to fight
They will push past their demons
And decide to live
Your story will be a healing manual
Proof that you made it
And others can, too
Your story will be a call to arms
Giving others the courage to step forward
A light in the darkness
Your story deserves to be shared
A reckoning
Let your heart spill, your truth unfurl
Your words cleanse
Let others bask in your resilience
Bring comfort to others
And let them bring comfort to you
Call out to your army of fellow survivors
Give voice to the voiceless
Someone, somewhere will hear your story
And decide to fight
Let your voice ring out loud

Survivor

I am not a victim
I have picked up the pieces of my life
And put them back together

I am not alone
I walk in solidarity
With thousands of others like me

I am not weak
What has not killed me
Has made me stronger

I am not a statistic;
Not a number, but flesh and bones
Not a scare tactic, but a human being

I am not a victim
I am a survivor

Because of You

Because of you, I lived in fear
Because of me, I found courage
Because of you, I was lost in the dark
Because of me, I made my way
Into the light
You thought I was weak,
I proved my strength
You tried to silence me,
I demanded to be heard
You tried to stomp my spirit,
I rose too high for you to reach
Because of you,
My life was forever changed
Because of me, I am finding purpose
In this new life of mine
Because of you, all I knew was pain
Because of me, I am basking in love
Because of you, I am broken
Because of me,
I am beautiful at the broken parts